SLENDER ACTIFRY
COOKBOOK

SLENDER ACTIFRY COOKBOOK

By Maryanne Madden

Slender Actifry Cookbook by Maryanne Madden, Published by Maryanne Madden.

www.maryannemadden.com

Cover by Maryanne Scott

FREE COOKBOOK DOWNLOAD

25 low calorie curry recipes for your slow cooker with easy to follow instructions. Delicious recipes

Would like a free cookbook for your slow cooker?

I'm currently writing a new cookbook, "Slender Slow Cooker Curry Cookbook" and I'm offering a taster of the book for free on my website.

Visit this link: http://www.maryannemadden.com/slender-cookbooks

INTRODUCTION

The Actifry is much more than a low fat chip fryer. It will revolutionise your cooking and is great for low calorie dieters. Just imagine being able to simply put your food into it and walk away?

Just One tbsp. of olive oil over your uncooked chips, switch it on, walk away and come back 40 minutes later to perfectly cooked chips every time.

You can brown your minced beef, cook meatballs, roast your vegetables without basting turning or watching the clock?

You just don't need to watch it - the Actifry does all these things on automatic while you get on with other jobs. It's like having a kitchen assistant stirring the pot for you.

This cookbook is for you if:

* You're following a healthy low calorie diet.

* You want to look and feel fantastic.

* You love fried food but don't want to eat unhealthily (don't we all...)

* You don't want to spend all your time in the kitchen. It's easy to put the ingredients together in one dish and create a quick and tasty meal.

I hope you enjoy the recipes and make some positive progress with your weight loss journey.

Maryanne Madden

PS ... Don't forget to request my popular **FREE REPORT** for some brilliant proven weight loss tips that actually work. Be one of the hundreds who have already benefited from the fantastic guide.

DISCLAIMER

I am not a doctor, dietician or nutritionist. I am not offering a professional opinion, or scientific data. This is simply my guide to low calorie eating. You should always consult with your doctor prior to starting a new diet if at all concerned.

I make no claims as to whether these recipes will work for you, but I do ask that you enjoy the recipes and don't give yourself a hard time if the particular diet you're following isn't working (despite your best efforts). There are no quick wins, its important to make simple life style changes and follow a healthy eating plan.

HOW TEFAL ACTIFRY WORKS

Tefal ActiFry's patented hot air system and unique stirring paddle ensure food is cooked through evenly.

New this year, the Actifry 2-in-1 allows you to cook two separate dishes in one appliance at the same time.

The ActiFry needs no pre-heating, and a constant cooking temperature of approximately 170°C guarantees crispy chips every time.

The removable ceramic-coated pan is easy to clean and dishwasher safe - as are the paddle and lid.

The range of sizes suits all families: from the 1kg capacity model, which serves up to four large portions, through to the 1.5kg model, serving up to six people.

How does it work?

It works with a combination of convection heat from the unit in the lid and a paddle, which stirs the contents around, coating them in a thin layer of oil and allowing everything to have its share of the cooking heat

How to clean it?

The best thing about the Actifry is that the base, stirrer and lid all go in the dishwasher. And as most of the oil is absorbed but you only put a tsp in anyway so there isn't mush to be left.

HANDY HINTS

Don't add salt to chips while the chips are in the pan. Only add salt once the chips are removed from the appliance at the end of cooking.

When adding dried herbs and spices to Actifry, mix them with some oil or liquid. If you try sprinkling them directly into the pan the hot air system will just blow them around.

For best results, use finely chopped garlic instead of crushed garlic to avoid it adhering to the central paddle.

Strong coloured spices may slightly stain the paddle and parts of the appliance. This is normal.

If using onions in Actifry recipes, they are best thinly sliced instead of chopped as they cook better. Separate the onion the rings before adding them to the pan and give them a quick stir so that they are evenly distributed.

With meat and poultry dishes, stop the appliance and stir the pan once or twice during cooking so that the food on top does not dry out and the dish thickens evenly.

Prepare vegetables in small pieces or stir fry size to ensure they cook through.

COOKING GUIDE

Potatoes

	Type	Qty	Oil	Time
Chips	Fresh	1000g (unpeeled)	1 tbs oil	40-45 mins
	Fresh	750g	½ spoonful oil	35-37 mins
	Fresh	500g	½ spoonful oil	28-30 mins
	Fresh	250g	½ spoonful oil	24-26 mins
Potatoes (quartered)	Fresh	1000g	1 tbs oil	40-42 mins
Diced	Fresh	1000g	1 tbs oil	40-42 mins
Chips	Frozen	750g	None	35-40 mins

Meat

	Type	Qty	Oil	Time
Chicken	Fresh	750g	None	10-15 mins
Lamb/Pork Chops	Fresh	2-6	None	20-25 mins
Sausages	Fresh	4-8	None	10-12 mins
Beef steak	Fresh	600g	None	8-10 mins

Fish

	Type	Qty	Oil	Time
Cod Haddock	Fresh	500g	1 tbsp.	20-22 mins
King Prawns	Frozen or fresh	300g	None	12-14 mins

ABOUT LOW CALORIE DIETS

A low calorie diet, which might also be called a calorie restricted diet, provides a simple way to lose weight and is usually an important part of weight loss plans such as those used by slimming clubs.

We all know that all food has a calorific value; it's on food packaging the world over. We also know that we need to eat a certain amount of calories everyday to survive.

So how do you determine how many calories you should be eating to lose weight?

If you visit www.myfitnesspal.com or Google "how many calories should I be eating" there are plenty of places that will tell you how many calories you should be eating to lose weight, based on your current weight, age, height and level of activity.

Once you have your number, you're good to go!

Is there really such a thing as good or bad calories?

Basically yes, though this is just guide so feel free to ignore me completely.

Obviously you would be better getting your calories from wholesome food, like vegetables, lean meat and whole grains; however in the real world, we like wine, and chocolate and pizza. Just remember "Everything in moderation"!

INTERESTING DIET INFORMATION

The aim of the book is to provide tasty recipes under 500, 400, 300 and 200 calories (even a few sneaky recipes under 100). You'll find some that include butter, sugar and cream. Don't let that put you off.

A little bit of fat in your diet isn't necessarily a bad thing. However if you feel that the calories in the recipe are still too high for your calorie allowance, consider swapping the cuts of meat to those with fewer calories or swap the ingredients for lower calorie alternatives.

Remember

Chicken & fish have fewer calories than red meat like beef or lamb.

Filling up with fresh, steamed or boiled vegetables will keep you feeling full.

Removing all skins from chicken will reduce calories further.

Please give us your feedback

If you enjoy any of the recipes from this cookbook we'd really appreciate your feedback. Reviews help others decide if the book is the right one to choose, and also help us to get our cookbooks more widely recognized.

Click here to leave a review or to get in touch with the author visit http://www.maryannemadden.com

CONTENTS

RECIPES

Prawns & Celery

Serve: 2
294 Calories per serving

Ingredients

3 clove of Garlic, finely chopped
6 to 8 stalks of Celery, sliced diagonally
½ Carrot, sliced
10 to 12 Fresh Tiger Prawns
1 Tbsp. of Olive Oil
1 tbsp. Oyster Sauce
1 tsp Sugar
1 tsp Cornflour
200ml of Water

Instructions

Place the garlic, celery and carrot into the Actifry and pour in 1 Tbsp. of olive oil. Then set the timer to 8 minutes.

In a large bowl, mix the oyster sauce, light soya sauce, sugar, cornflour and water.

Add the mixture into the Actifry and after the 8 minutes add in the shrimps and set the timer for another 5 minutes.

Prawn & Potatoes

Serve: 4
339 Calories per serving

Ingredients

800 g baby new potatoes unpeeled
2 garlic cloves of garlic
1-½ Tbsp. light olive oil
4 tomatoes, skinned, seeded and chopped
12 raw, peeled prawns
Salt and freshly ground black pepper, to taste

Instructions

Rinse the potatoes thoroughly (keeping the skins on) then drain and dry them well and place them into the ActiFry pan.

Separate the cloves of garlic without removing the skins, and add the garlic cloves to the ActiFry.

Drizzle the oil evenly over the potatoes and garlic and cook for 20 minutes.

Add the tomatoes to the Actifry and cook for another 10 minutes,

Finally add the prawns and seasoning to the Actifry and cook for a further 5 minutes or until the prawns are cooked.

Serve with a crisp green salad.

Sweet Potato

Serve: 1
183 Calories per serving

Ingredients

1 sweet potato per person
Salt n pepper to season
2 tsp olive oil

Instructions

First remove the paddle from Actifry

Prick the sweet potatoes and rub with a little oil and season to taste with salt & pepper.

Place into the Actifry and cook for 45 minutes.

Serve with low fat soured cream, jalapenos, and chopped coriander.

Beef and Broccoli

Serve: 4
422 Calories per serving

Ingredients

2 tbsp. - Cornflour
200ml - Water, plus
2 tbsp. - Water
1/2 tsp - Minced Garlic
340g Sirloin Steak, cut width ways into 6mm wide strips
1 ½ Tbsp. - Vegetable oil, divided
105g - Broccoli florets
1 - Small Onion, cut into wedges
80g - Soy Sauce
2 tbsp. - Brown sugar
1 tsp - Ground Ginger

Instructions

In a bowl, combine 1 ½ tbsp. Cornflour, 1 tbsp. water and the Minced Garlic and mix until smooth.

Add the beef to this mixture and leave to marinate for 2 hours (or as long as you feel).

Add the beef and ½ Tbsp. of Oil, to the Actifry and cook for 10 minutes. Then set the beef to one side.

Next add the broccoli, Onion, and another Tbsp. of Oil and cook for 8 minutes.

In another bowl, combine the Ginger, Brown Sugar, Soy Sauce and the remaining Cornflour and water.

Add beef and Sauce mixture back into the Actifry and cook for 6 mins.

Bacon, Leek & potato

Serve: 2
334 Calories per serving

Ingredients

200g new potatoes, diced
½ leek sliced
2 smoked bacon medallions, chopped
1 tsp oil
1/2 tsp smoked paprika
2 Poached Eggs

Instructions

Dice the potatoes and slice the leek and add 1 Tbsp. of oil and cook for 10 minutes.

Next add the bacon, paprika and spinach and cook for another few minutes (or until the bacon is cooked and the spinach wilted).

Serve with a poached egg.

Bolognaise

Serve: 2
290 Calories per serving

Ingredients

500g minced beef (5% fat)
1-diced carrot
1 stick of celery
300g Fresh tomatoes
½ white onion sliced
2 tbsp. olive oil
Pinch of salt

Instructions

Put the olive oil into the Actifry for 1 minute.

Next add the vegetables and the beef and cook for 10 minutes.

In a blender, blend the tomatoes into a puree and then add them to the meat and vegetables in the ActiFry.

Season with salt and cook for 20 minutes more.

{HANDY TIP – Add a little chilli powder and some red kidney beans for a quick chilli-con-carne}

Breaded cauliflower

Serve: 2
181 Calories per serving

Ingredients

1 cauliflower
20g Flour
1 Large Egg
30g breadcrumbs
1 tbsp. of oil

Instructions

Cut the cauliflower into small florets and boil for 5 minutes (the cauliflower should still be crunchy)

After boiling, drain, then cover the small florets with flour and then dip in egg, then breadcrumbs.

Remove the paddle from the ActiFry and then add the coated (you may have to do 2 or 3 batches).

Sprinkle with 1 tbsp. of oil, cook for 15 minutes, then add the paddle and cook for another 5 minutes or until golden brown.

Cajun chicken

Serve: 4
397 Calories per serving

Ingredient

1 tsp Cajun Spice
450g of chicken wings
1 tbsp. of olive oil

Instruction

Remove any skin from the chicken wings.

In a large bowl, mix the Cajun spices with the chicken wings until they are completely covered.

Place chicken wings in ActiFry and add the 1tbs of oil.

Cook for 35 minutes.

Chicken curry

Serve: 4
484 Calories per serving

Ingredients

1 red Pepper
1 white Onions,
1 lb. Diced chicken
205g Chopped tomatoes
100ml Single cream
1 tsp Curry paste.

Instructions

Cut your peppers and onions and add to ActiFry for ten minutes

In a large bowl combine the diced chicken and curry paste and mix together.

Add diced chicken to ActiFry and cook for 15 minutes.

Finally add the chopped tomatoes for 5 minutes then add the single cream and cook for a further 5 minutes.

{HANDY TIP – Serve with cauliflower cous-cous instead of rice to save on calories}

Chicken nuggets

Serve: 2
369 Calories per serving

Ingredients

2 boneless, skinless chicken breast.

Marinade
120ml low fat buttermilk
½ tsp of Garlic powder
½ tsp of Onion powder

Coating
90g breadcrumbs
½ tsp of Garlic powder
½ tsp of Onion powder
½ tsp of seasoning salt
½ tsp of lemon pepper
½ tsp of paprika

Instructions

Cut 2 chicken breast into small pieces and then place into a large bowl, pour enough cream to cover and add the remainder of the marinade ingredients. Marinade for at least 30 minutes.

Mix breadcrumbs, garlic powder, onion powder salt, lemon pepper and Paprika in a large bowl and dredge chicken in it to coat.

Place the chicken into the ActiFry with 1 tbsp. of oil, and cook for 15 minutes.

Salsa Chicken

Serve: 2
346 Calories per serving

Ingredients

1 Tbsp. Olive oil
450g Skinless, chicken
1 tbsp. Salsa

Instructions

Add 1 Tbsp. of olive oil into the Actifry and heat for 1 minute.

Cut the chicken into bite size pieces and put in the Actifry to cook for 15 min or until almost done.

Finally add the salsa heat through, for 2 more minutes.

Serve with a fresh green salad.

Chicken & Pineapple

Serve: 3
398 Calories per serving

Ingredients

600 g skinless boneless chicken breasts, cut into thin strips
1 spoon cornflour, plus extra to coat the chicken strips
2 tbsp. sunflower oil
250 g tinned pineapple pieces (drained weight) in natural juice, drained
(reserve the juice)
2 tbsp. Light soy sauce
½ tbsp. ground ginger
½ tbsp. mild curry powder
250 ml cold water
1/2-1 tbsp. sweetener

Instructions

In a large bowl, lightly coat the strips of chicken with a mixture of cornflour, salt and pepper.

Place the chicken in the ActiFry and then drizzle the oil evenly over the chicken and cook for 5 minutes.

In a large bowl mix the ground ginger, curry powder and pineapple pieces with the soy sauce, then pour this over the chicken, and then add the water and sweetener.

Mix 1 Tbsp. of cornflour with the pineapple juice in a small bowl, until smooth. Add this to the ActiFry.

Cook for a further 10 minutes, or until the chicken is cooked and tender.

Chilli chips

Serve: 2
147 Calories per serving

Ingredients

800g new potatoes
1 tbsp. Chilli powder (mild or hot)

Instructions

Cut the new potatoes into chips (leave skin on)

Add the oil over the chips then sprinkle with the chilli powder.

Cook for 30-40 minutes.

Chilli con Carne

Serve: 4
420 Calories per serving

Ingredients

400g Lean minced beef (5% fat)
1-diced carrot
1 stick of celery 300g of peeled tomatoes
1/2 white onion sliced
2 tbsp. of extra virgin olive oil pinch of salt
1 tbsp. Chilli powder
205g Red Kidney Beans

Instructions

Put the extra virgin olive oil to heat in the ActiFry for 1 minute

Add the vegetables and the meat, and cook for 10 minutes

Blend the peeled tomatoes into a puree and then add them to the meat and vegetables in the ActiFry.

Season with salt and cook for about 20 minutes.

{HANDY TIP - Serve with cauliflower rice to save on calories}

Coronation Chicken

Serve: 1
465 Calories per serving

Ingredients

150g diced chicken breast
2 tbsp.s of lite mayonnaise
2 tbsp.s of peas
30g of apricots that have been soaked in 75mls of boiling water
3 tsps of medium curry powder
20g of whole blanched almonds

Instructions

First add the almonds to the Actifry and cook for 5 minutes.

Then add the chicken to the almonds and cook for a further 2 minutes.

In a large bowl mix the apricots with 75mls of boiling water.

Then mix in the mayonnaise and curry powder and add to the Actifry.

Cook for at least 12 minutes and then add the peas and cook for a further 2 minutes

Spicy Prawns & Vegetables

Serve: 1
439 Calories per serving

Ingredients

1 onion, thinly sliced
1 fresh red chilli, seeded and thinly sliced
1 clove garlic, finely chopped
2 tsp sunflower oil
2 courgettes cut diagonally into 3 mm (1/8 in) slices
100 g mangetout, trimmed
75 ml cold water
85g cooked, tiger prawns
3 spring onions, thinly sliced or chopped
1 spoon chopped fresh coriander, plus extra to garnish
2 tbsp.s black bean sauce

Instructions

Place the onion, chilli, and garlic in the ActiFry and then drizzle the oil over the top and cook for 5 minutes.

Next add the courgettes, mangetout and water to the ActiFry. Cook for a further 5 minutes.

Finally add the prawns, spring onions, chopped coriander and black bean sauce and cook for 3 minutes.

Sprinkle with chopped coriander to serve.

Hot & Spicy King Prawns

Serve: 2
371 Calories per serving

Ingredients

450g large raw King prawns, shelled and deveined
2 tbsp. olive oil
2 tbsp. water
1 tsp Tabasco sauce
1-tsp red pepper flakes
1 tsp dried oregano
½ tsp dried parsley
½ tsp pepper
½ tsp garlic powder
½ tsp onion salt
½ tsp smoked paprika

Instructions

Place all ingredients except for prawns in a large bowl and mix well.

Add the shrimp and marinate in the fridge for 4 to 6 hours.

Remove prawns from the marinade and add to the ActiFry, then cook for 10 minutes, (or until they are pink).

Serve with a crunchy salad.

Curried Tofu

Serve: 2
334 Calories per serving

Ingredients

1 tbsp. olive oil
1 tbsp. mild Indian-style curry paste
75g chopped onion
75g red pepper
1 clove garlic, minced
½ tbsp. minced fresh ginger
450g firm tofu, cubed
75g frozen peas
125 ml vegetable broth
2 tbsp. raisins
2 chopped fresh coriander

Instructions

In a bowl mix the olive oil with the curry paste.

Add the oil mixture, onion, red pepper, garlic and ginger to the ActiFry and cook for about 3 minutes.

Next add the cubed tofu to the ActiFry and cook for 5 minutes.

Then add the peas, broth and raisins and then cook for 4 minutes or until peas are tender.

Finally sprinkle with coriander.

Chicken with strawberry salsa

Serve: 4
357 Calories per serving

Ingredients

600g chicken thighs, skin removed, trimmed
1-tbsp extra-virgin olive oil
3 tbsp. chopped fresh oregano
2 1/2 tbsp. chopped fresh chives, divided
½ -tsp salt plus a pinch, divided
1/4 tsp freshly ground pepper plus a pinch, divided
400g strawberries, hulled and chopped
2 tsp freshly grated lime zest
1 tsp sugar, or to taste
1 tsp balsamic vinegar, or more to taste

Instructions

Combine chicken in a bowl with oil, oregano, 1 tbsp. chives, ½ tsp salt and

1/4 tsp pepper and leave marinade for 1 hour.

Place the Chicken in ActiFry and cook for 35 minutes.

Next in a large bowl combine strawberries, lime zest, sugar, vinegar, the

remaining 1 1/2 tbsp.s chives and the remaining pinch of salt and pepper.

Serve the chicken with the relish.

Honeyed chicken

Serve: 2
451 Calories per serving

Ingredients

500g Chicken Breast
1tsp Dried Chilli Flakes
3 cloves garlic
1tsp Sea salt Black pepper
100g runny honey
Fresh green salad

Instructions

In a bowl mix the garlic, dried chilli, honey, salt and pepper.

Cut the chicken into bite size pieces and put in Actifry with 1 spoon of oil.

Cook for 15 minutes, and when Chicken starting to brown, add the honey mixture and mix thoroughly.

Cook for the remaining few minutes and serve with a fresh green salad.

Lemon Chicken

Serve: 2
340 Calories per serving

Ingredients

450g chicken breast
1 tbsp. vegetable oil
50ml lemon juice from concentrate
50ml soy sauce
½ tsp garlic powder
Lemon pepper

Instructions

In a large bowl, mix the vegetable oil, lemon juice, soy sauce and garlic powder.

Add the wings and mix together to coat the chicken breast, then marinate for a few hours (or overnight if possible).

Remove wings from marinade and place in the Actifry.

Cook for 40 minutes, or until cooked through.

Sprinkle with lemon pepper and serve with a salad of your choice.

Chicken Madras

Serve: 1
468 Calories per serving

Ingredients

1 large chicken breast (chopped)
1 medium sized onion chopped
1 crushed garlic clove
1 tbsp. of olive oil, or groundnut oil
1 tsp of cumin
1 tsp of turmeric
2 tomatoes, peeled and chopped
1 tbsp. of desiccated coconut
1 tbsp. of ground coriander
1-2 tsp of mild curry powder (according to taste)
300mls of chicken stock.

Instructions

Add the chopped chicken and half of the olive oil to the Actifry and cook for 5 minutes.

Next add the chopped onion and crushed garlic to the Actifry and continue to cook for a further 5 minutes.

In a separate bowl, mix the spices and coconut with the remaining olive oil and add to the chicken mixture.

Allow to cook for a further 10 minutes before adding the tomatoes and chicken stock.

Cook for a further 8 minutes, adding a little water if necessary.

{HANDY TIP – Serve with cauliflower rice instead of Basmati rice to save on calories}

Meatballs & Potatoes

Serve: 3
316 Calories per serving

Ingredients

500g lean minced beef (pre-made meatballs, frozen)
1 tbsp. olive oil
2 medium potatoes cubed
½ large sweet potato cubed
½ chopped onion
1 sliced celery stick
80g sliced mushroom
40g chopped red pepper
1 tsp garlic salt & pepper

Instructions

Add the frozen meatballs to the Actifry with 1 tbsp. of olive oil.

Cut potato, and sweet potato into large cubes and put in to the ActiFry season well with garlic plus, seasoning salt and pepper and cook for 20 minutes.

Next add onions, mushrooms, celery and cook for another 10 minutes.

Veggie hash

Serve: 1
356 Calories per serving

Ingredients

1 chopped red onion.
1 diced red pepper
1 chopped courgette
1 diced yellow pepper
Small handful of mange tout
A quarter of butternut squash, chopped
1 carrot, chopped small
2 whole garlic cloves
2 tbsp.s of olive oil
1 tsp of tomato puree

Instructions

Add the onion, peppers, butternut squash, carrot and oil to the Actifry and cook for 5 minutes.

Then add the tomato puree, whole garlic cloves, mange tout and courgette and cook for another 10 minutes.

Add a little water and then cook for a further 10 minutes until the vegetables are tender.

Tarragon Chicken

Serve: 2
428 Calories per serving

Ingredients

2 boneless chicken breasts, skinned & diced
125g sliced mushrooms
300ml chicken stock
1/2 Tbsp. of cornflour
1 sprig fresh tarragon, finely chopped
100ml low fat cream
50g shallots, sliced thinly
1 Tbsp. of oil
Salt & pepper

Instructions

Heat the Actifry & add the chicken pieces (seasoned with salt and pepper).

Cook for about 3 minutes and then add the shallots & mushrooms and cook for another 7 minutes.

In a bowl, mix the stock, cornflower and cream and then add it to the Actifry, coating everything.

Cook for another 2-3 minutes & then add the chopped tarragon.

Peanut & Chicken Curry

Serve: 6
476 Calories per serving

Ingredients

1 kg chicken breast (cubed)
1 spoon oil
55g red curry paste
400ml can lite coconut milk
55g fish sauce
2 spoons sugar
½ cup lite crunchy peanut butter

Instructions

Heat oil in Actifry for 3 minutes.

Place the cubed chicken breast into the Actifry and cook for 5 minutes.

Next add the red curry paste and cook for a further 5 minutes.

In the meantime, combine coconut milk, fish sauce, sugar and peanut

butter in a bowl and add to the Actifry, then cook for a further 15 minutes.

Lime chicken

Serve: 2
228 Calories per serving

Ingredients

500g Chicken breast (chopped)
Juice of one small lime
1 tsp olive oil
Salt & Pepper

Instructions

Place chopped chicken breast in the ActiFry.

Sprinkle with the oil, lime juice, salt & pepper.

Cook for 25 minutes and then serve with a green salad.

Rosemary & Garlic Potatoes

Serve: 2
375 Calories per serving

Ingredients

800g Baby New Potatoes
1 tbsp. Olive oil infused with rosemary
3 Cloves Garlic
1 tbsp. Dry Rosemary
Sea Salt

Instructions

Chop the new potatoes in half and add to the Actifry with the garlic cloves.

Cover with 1 tbsp. of oil.

Cook for for 40 mins and then sprinkle with sea salt to serve.

Salmon and mushroom

Serve: 4
292 Calories per serving

Ingredients

4 Boneless Salmon Fillets (Cut in half)
500g Mushrooms cut into bite-sized pieces
1 tbsp. Olive oil
Rocket Leaves

Instructions

Place all the ingredients into the Actifry and drizzle with tbsp. of oil.one

Cook for 10 minutes and then serve on a bed of rocket salad.

Season to taste.

Salmon and pesto

Serve: 1
310 Calories per serving

Ingredients

1 Fresh salmon fillet,
1 tbsp. pesto sauce
1 tbsp. breadcrumbs

Instructions

Spread a thin layer of pesto on top of the salmon fillet, and cover with breadcrumbs.

Remove the paddle from the Actifry and cook for 8 minutes or until the topping is crispy.

Serve with a green salad.

Chinese Salt & Pepper chicken

Serve: 3
312 Calories per serving

Ingredients

40g plain flour
¼ tsp Chinese five spice
1 and 1/4 tsp salt
¾ tsp white pepper
3 chicken fillets cut into strips
2 cloves of garlic
2 tsp fresh chilli
2 spring onions chopped.

Instructions

In a bowl mix the flour salt, pepper and five spices.

Place the chicken into the bowl to coat it.

Place in the ActiFry for about 20 minutes or till chicken is cooked through.

Finally add ½ clove of garlic, fresh chilli and spring onions and cook for further 5 minutes.

Scallops & Potatoes

Serve: 2
277 Calories per serving

Ingredients

600g scallops
1 bunch of asparagus (about 1 pound)
55g-diced shallot
2 tbsp. olive oil
1 fresh chopped thyme leaves
2 tsp finely grated lemon zest
½ tsp salt
¼ tsp freshly ground black pepper
2 fresh lemon juice

Instructions

Rinse the scallops and pat dry.

Next trim the asparagus and cut into diagonal 3 cm pieces.

Place the diced shallots into the ActiFry and drizzle with ½ tbsp. of oil and cook for 3 minutes.

Then add the thyme, lemon zest, asparagus, scallops salt and pepper.

Drizzle with the remaining oil and cook for a further 9 minutes or until the scallops are cooked and the asparagus is crisp.

Drizzle with the lemon juice and serve.

Beans & Sausage

Serve: 4
425 Calories per serving

Ingredients

8 Low fat sausages
4 Potatoes
1 Large tin baked beans

Instructions

Cube the potatoes and add to the ActiFry.

Next, cut each sausage into 4 and add to the ActiFry

Cook for 25 minutes and then add in the baked beans.

Heat for a further 3 minutes.

Sausage & Bean Cassolet

Serve: 4
285 Calories per serving

Ingredients

450 g pork sausages
1 large onion, thinly sliced
1 spoon sunflower oil (if required)
410 g cannellini beans, rinsed and drained
400 g tin chopped tomatoes
150 ml dry cider
1 tbsp. caster sugar
1 tbsp. dried mixed herbs
Salt and freshly ground black pepper, to taste
Chopped fresh parsley, to garnish

Instructions

Place the sausages in the ActiFry and cook for 10 minutes.

Next add the sliced onion and cook for 5 minutes.

Add the beans, tomatoes, cider, sugar, dried herbs and seasoning and cook

for 10 minutes,

Garnish with chopped parsley.

{HANDY TIP – Use Apple juice instead of cider if you prefer}

Spicy steak

Serve: 1
454 Calories per serving

Ingredients

600g Sirloin steak
500g small white mushrooms
500ml Diet Coke
2 tbsp. minced garlic
2 tsp Cajun spice mix
2 tsp crushed chilli
1 Tbsp. Basil olive oil
Salt and pepper to taste

Instructions

In a large bowl add the diet coke, garlic, Cajun spice and chilli.

Cut the steak into 2-3cm cubes and add to the marinade. Leave overnight if possible.

Heat the Basil oil in the Actifry for 1 minute and then add the steak and cook for 5 mins

Finally add the mushrooms and cook for another 10 minutes.

Thai Chicken

Serve: 4
321 Calories per serving

Ingredients

450g boneless, skinless chicken breast, sliced into thin strips
1 tsp minced fresh gingerroot
½ tsp each salt and pepper
1 garlic glove, minced
1 small red chili pepper, seeded and chopped
2 Tbsp. groundnut oil
1 each red and green pepper, thinly sliced
1 medium-size courgette, sliced
125ml lite coconut milk
2 tsp cornflour
1 tsp green Thai curry paste
2 tbsp. chopped fresh coriander

Instructions

In a bowl, mix the chicken strips, gingerroot, salt, pepper, chili pepper and garlic with half of the oil.

Mix well and then add to the Actifry and cook for 8 minutes.

Remove the chicken and place to one side.

Next add the peppers, courgette and remaining oil to the ActiFry and cook for 5 minutes.

In the meantime, whisk the coconut milk with the cornflour and curry paste until smooth.

Add this mixture and the chicken to the ActiFry and cook for 5 minutes.

Finally stir in the coriander.

Stuffed Peppers

Serve: 3
300 Calories per serving

Ingredients

500g Mince Beef
1 large onion
3 tbsp. Taco seasoning
6 red peppers

Instructions

Add the mince, finely chopped onion and taco seasoning to the Actifry and cook for about 10-12 minutes.

Slice the tops off the peppers, and remove the seeds.

Stuff with the mince mixture and then replace the pepper tops.

Remove the paddle from the Actifry and cook for about 15 minutes.

Watch carefully to ensure they don't burn, then remove and serve.

Sweet & Savoury Turkey

Serve: 4
424 Calories per serving

Ingredients

400 g boneless turkey breast, cut in cubes
350g pumpkin cut into cubes
4 tbsp. maple syrup
1 sliced onion
1 bay leaf
1 sprig fresh thyme chopped
½ tbsp. nutmeg
6 tbsp. cranberry sauce
300ml low-fat chicken stock
1 tbsp. olive oil
Salt and pepper

Instructions

Heat the oil in the ActiFry for 1 minute and then add the onion, the turkey pieces and brown for 5 minutes.

Next add the maple syrup and cook for a few minutes until it begins to caramelize.

Then add the pumpkin and nutmeg and cook for 2 minutes.

After 2 minutes add the chicken stock and the herbs and cook for 15 minutes.

Finally stir in the cranberry sauce and cook for another 2 minutes.

Turmeric Chicken

Serve: 4
256 Calories per serving

Ingredients

500g Chicken Breasts (approx. 4)
3 tbsp. Turmeric powder
1 tbsp. of Salt

Instructions

Cut a crisscross pattern into the chicken breasts with a sharp knife.

Rub with turmeric powder and salt.

Place in the fridge for at least an hour and then put in the Actifry.

Cook for 30 minutes or until it turns brown.

Serve on a bed of peppery rocket salad.

Spicy Vegetables

Serve: 1
337 Calories per serving

Ingredients

1 medium sized chopped onion
1 crushed clove of garlic (or squeeze of garlic puree)
1 tbsp. of olive oil or rapeseed oil
Handful of chopped mushrooms (any type)
Quarter of a butternut squash, peeled and diced
100mls of vegetable stock
1 tsp of chilli powder
1 tsp of cumin
Salt and Pepper
Half a courgette, diced.
1 tomato peeled and chopped

Instructions

First add the onion and garlic to the Actifry and cook for 2 minutes.

In a separate bowl, mix the spices with the olive oil and add to the onion mixture, then cook for a further 2 minutes

Next add the diced butternut squash, mushrooms and vegetable stock and cook for 5 minutes.

Finally add the tomato and courgette and a little boiling water and season with salt and pepper.

Cook for 5 minutes and then serve.

Butternut Squash Ristotto

Serve: 4
386 Calories per serving

Ingredients

1 medium onion, finely sliced
70g pack pancetta cubes
350g peeled butternut squash, cut into 2cm pieces
250g Arborio risotto rice
2 garlic cloves, finely chopped
1.6 litres hot chicken stock
Handful fresh parsley, chopped
2 tbsp. Mascarpone

Instructions

Put the onion, pancetta, squash, rice and garlic into the ActiFry and cook for 5 minutes.

Stir in 1 litre of the stock and cook for 40min.

Add the mascarpone, remaining 600ml stock and some seasoning and cook for a further 20min.

Stir through the parsley and serve.

Zesty Chilli Chicken

Serve: 3
399 Calories per serving

Ingredients

3 cubed Chicken Breasts
1 red chilli, deseeded and chopped finely
3 lemons (juice and zest)
3 cloves of garlic. Finely chopped
1 onion thinly sliced
200g new potatoes
12 cherry tomatoes, halved
2 tbsp.s olive oil

Instructions

In a large bowl, mix the chicken, chilli, garlic, onion, lemon juice and zest, 1 tbsp. of the oil, and then place in the fridge for 1 hour.

Put the potatoes in the ActiFry, drizzle with 1 tbsp. of the oil, cook for 15 minutes.

Then add the chicken mixture and cook for a further 15 minutes.

Finally add the cherry tomatoes and cook for a further 5 minutes.

Serve with a slice of lemon.

Corned Beef Hash

Serve: 4
429 Calories per serving

Ingredients

5 medium potatoes peeled and diced
1 onion, peeled and chopped
1 large carrot, peeled and crated
1 tin corned beef (low fat), chopped into cubes
205g Baked beans
1 tbsp. Olive oil

Instructions

Add the potato to the Actifry with 1 tbsp. of olive oil and cook for 5 minutes.

Next add the onions to the potatoes and cook for a further 10 minutes.

Finally add the grated carrot and corned beef and cook for 3 minutes

Serve with baked beans

Garlic Mushroom

Serve: 1
180 Calories per serving

Ingredients

400g Mushrooms, Washed, Chopped and Dried
2 Tsps Olive Oil
1 Clove of Garlic, Chopped
Chopped parsley to serve

Instructions

Chop the mushrooms roughly and add to the Actifry with the garlic

Add the olive oil and then cook for 10 minutes.

Sprinkle over the chopped parsley and serve.

Roasted Cauliflower

Serve: 2
79 Calories per serving

Ingredients

1 head of cauliflower
1tsp olive oil
1tsp mild or medium curry powder
Juice from half a lemon
Sea salt and black pepper

Instructions

Wash the cauliflower, remove the leaves and the core, and then break into similar size pieces.

Put the oil into the Actifry, and heat for 2 minutes.

Then add the lemon juice, curry powder, and stir to mix with the oil.

Finally add the cauliflower and salt and pepper.

Cook for 20 minutes, or until crispy on the outside and just starting to brown.

Chicken Tikka Masala

Serve: 4
457 Calories per serving

Ingredients

500g Boneless, skinless chicken breasts, cut into 2cm pieces
100g Tikka Masala curry paste
300g Natural low fat yoghurt
1 Tbsp. vegetable oil
1 Large onion, finely chopped
390g tin of premium chopped tomatoes
150ml Water
½ Tsp sugar
2 Tsp fresh lemon juice
1 Bunch coriander leaves, chopped

Instructions

In a large bowl mix the chicken, curry paste and yoghurt.

Cover and leave in the fridge to marinade over night (or for at least 2 hours).

Heat the oil in your Actifry for 2 minutes then add the onion and cook for 5 minutes.

Add the chicken and cook for another 10 minutes.

Add the tomatoes and water and cook for another 10 minutes.

Add the yoghurt, sugar and lemon juice. Stir well and cook for another 5 minutes.

Serve sprinkled with fresh coriander

Full English Breakfast

Serve: 1
484 Calories per serving

Ingredients

2 low fat sausages
2-3 rashes of smoked bacon chopped
1 small potato cut into cubes
A few mushrooms chopped into chunks
Half a tin of baked beans
Half a tin of chopped tomatoes
1 Egg, poached or fried

Instructions

First cook the sausages & potatoes for 10 minutes in the Actifry (Without additional oil).

Then added the chopped bacon for a further 10 minutes.

Next add the mushrooms & cook for around 5 minutes.

Finally add the baked beans & tomatoes and cook for another 2 minutes.

Poach an egg separately and serve with the breakfast.

French Chicken

Serve: 4
397 Calories per serving

Ingredients

225g boneless chicken breasts, skinned & diced
125g sliced mushrooms
300ml chicken stock
½ tbsp. of instant mash
1 sprig fresh tarragon, finely chopped
100ml Quark
50g shallots, sliced thinly
1 tbsp. Olive oil
Salt & pepper

Instructions

Heat the Actifry for 1 minute then add the chicken pieces and then cook for 3 minutes.

Add the shallots & mushrooms and season with salt & pepper, and then cook for 7 minutes.

Next add the chicken stock, mixed with the mash & the quark, and cook for another 2-3 minutes.

Finally add the chopped tarragon and serve.

Chinese Pork

Serve: 4
458 Calories per serving

Ingredients

750g Pork loin, cut into sticks
1 1/2 Tbsp. of Soy sauce
1/2 tbsp. of sweetener
Frylight

Instructions

In a large bowl, mix the soy sauce, fry light & sweetener and marinate the pork in the mixture for at least 1 hour.

Place the marinated pork in the Actifry & spray with some fry light. Cook for 15 minutes.

Serve with a green salad.

Sirloin with wine

Serve: 2
500 Calories per serving

Ingredients

400g-sirloin steak
300g potatoes
1 red pepper
1 tbsp. of red wine
1 oregano, chopped
Frylight
1 tsp of cayenne chilli pepper

Instructions

Cut the steak into bite size pieces. Marinate in the red wine, with the oregano & the chili pepper.

Cut the potatoes into small pieces and put the potatoes & the peppers in the Actifry, add salt & spray with frylight & cook for 12 minutes.

Add the marinated meat, adjust the seasoning & cook for another 7 minutes.

Crispy Chicken

Serve: 1
325 Calories per serving

Ingredients

400g Chicken fillets
100g of Instant potato mix
2 medium eggs
1.5 tsp of chilli powder
1.5 tsp of salt
Frylight

Instructions

Butterfly the chicken breast and then cut long thin strips of abut 2cm in diameter.

In a bowl, crack the eggs and mix well, then add the instant mash to another bowl along with the dried spices and salt.

Dip each chicken strip in the egg and then in the crumb mix and onto a plate while you repeat the process for the rest of the chicken.

Spray both side of the strips with frylight, place into the ActiFry.

Cook for 15 minutes or until browned.

Vegetable Crisps

Serve: 1
256 Calories per serving

Ingredients

Frylight oil spray
1 carrot
1 parsnip
1 potato
Various seasonings (sea salt, pepper, paprika, garlic salt etc.)

Instructions

Heat the Actifry for 2 minutes.

Then thinly slice the root vegetables and spray with frylight.

Place into the Actifry and cook for 15 minutes or until beginning to crisp.

Season with salt, pepper or any other seasoning you choose.

Cauliflower Curry

Serve: 2
138 Calories per serving

Ingredients

1 small cauliflower
1 tsp curry powder
1 tbsp. vegetable oil
150g Fat free Greek yogurt
2 tsp sweetener
Season to taste
½ a cucumber (finely chopped)

Instructions

Cut the cauliflower into 1cm florets and place in the Actifry.

Sprinkle the curry powder evenly on top of the cauliflower and add the oil.

Cook for 20 minutes.

In a bowl, mix the sweetener & chopped cucumber into the yogurt.

Remove the cauliflower and serve with the dipping yogurt

Goat Cheese & Sun-dried Tomatoes Strips

Serve: 2
256 Calories per serving

Ingredients

115g fresh goat cheese
4 pieces sun-dried tomato
7 to 10 rocket leaves
1 sheet filo pastry

Instructions

Cut the filo pastry into 4 strips.

Place a ¼ of the fresh goat cheese on the end of each one.

Garnish the strips with a piece of sun-dried tomato.

Then add a few rocket leaves on top of each pastry strip and fold up into samosas.

Place in the Actifry and cook for 10 minutes.

Serve on a bed of rocket salad.

Italian Chicken

Serve: 2
252 Calories per serving

Ingredients

500g new potatoes
1 tbsp. of olive oil
2 chicken breast fillets
A green and red pepper
1 tin of tomatoes
1 Tsp of dried basil

Instructions

Take 500g of new potatoes and cut them into small chunks.

Put them in the Actifry, with 1 tbsp. of olive oil and cook for 20 minutes.

Chop two chicken breast fillets into medium size chunks.

Add them to the Actifry and cook for 5 minutes – (just enough to brown them).

Chop a green and red pepper into chunks – (cook for around 5 minutes.

Finally add a tin of chopped tomatoes, stir and add a tsp of dried basil.

Serve with a green salad

Chicken Fajitas

Serve: 2
307 Calories per serving

Ingredients

1 packet Fajitas powder
2 Onions
1 red peppers
4 chicken breast diced
½ tbsp. olive oil

Instructions

Slice the peppers and onions and put in Actifry with ½ tbsp. of oil and cook for 8 minutes.

Sprinkle the diced chicken breast with fajita powder.

Add the chicken to the ActiFry and cook for 15-20 minutes or until cooked.

Ratatouille

Serve: 2
234 Calories per serving

Ingredients

1 onion,
2 large ripe tomatoes,
1 Aubergine
1 Courgette
2 green peppers,
1 red pepper,
2 cloves garlic,
1 tbsp. olive oil,
Salt

Instructions

Dip the tomatoes in boiling water for a few seconds and then remove the skin and cut into cubes. Peel the aubergine and courgette.

Cut all the remaining ingredients (courgette, aubergine, peppers, garlic) in small pieces.

Add the oil to the Actifry and heat for 1 minute.

First cook the onion for 7 minutes, and then add the peppers, aubergine and courgette, and the tomatoes, and cook for 20 minutes.

Stuffed Garlic & Spinach Mushrooms

Serve: 4
218 Calories per serving

Ingredients:

8 Large Flat Field Mushrooms
1 tbs olive Oil
Salt and Pepper
4 Garlic Cloves
3 Large Tomatoes
170g Mozzarella Cheese
312g Baby Spinach

Instructions

First clean the mushrooms and remove the stalks.

Drizzle the oil over the mushrooms.

Place in the Actifry and gently cook for 5 minutes then turn them over.

Remove them from the Actifry and set to one side

In a bowl peel and crush the garlic, cut the tomatoes into 8 slices and grate the mozzarella.

Add the garlic and spinach and then place on top of each mushroom.

Place a tomato over each mushroom and sprinkle with the cheese.

Place in Actifry for 2-3 minutes or until bubbling. Serve immediately.

Potato Skins

Serve: 4
493 Calories per serving

Ingredients

3 Large baking potatoes
4-5 Strips of bacon
1 onion
200g Cheddar cheese
100ml Sour Cream
1 tbsp. Vegetable oil

Instructions

Wash and cut baking potatoes in half and with the oil.

Place the potatoes (cut side up) in the Actifry for 35 to 40 mins

For the last 10 minutes add sliced bacon.

Next chop the onions and grate the cheese and place to one side.

When the potatoes are ready, remove and scoop out the centre

Mix the potato centre with the sour cream and the bacon strips

Cover with the grated cheddar cheese and put back in the fryer for 5

minutes or until browned

Roasted Turnips

Serve: 1
158 Calories per serving

Ingredients

1 purple top turnip cubed
1 tbsp. olive oil or butter
¼ tsp. nutmeg
salt/pepper

Instructions

Clean and cube the turnip into 1-inch pieces

Place into ActiFry with 1 tbsp. of oil and salt and pepper to taste

Sprinkle a little nutmeg over the turnip

Cook for 35-40 minutes until soft and serve.

Spanish Potatoes

Serve: 4
368 Calories per serving

Ingredients

1 kg of potatoes
1 tbsp. of olive oil
1 tsp of smoked paprika
2 medium red onions
125 g chorizo.

Instructions

Peel the potatoes and cut into 2.5cm chunks and then place in the Actifry.

Mix the oil and paprika together and drizzle over the potatoes.

Switch on and leave to cook for about 45 minutes.

Meanwhile, peel and quarter the onions. Peel the chorizo and cut into small chunks.

After 45 minutes add the chorizo and onions and cook for a further 10 minutes.

Curried Salmon

Serve: 2
348 Calories per serving

Ingredients

400g cubes salmon
½ cucumber
4 g tsp green chilli
1/2 red onion
1 small tomato
1 ½ tbsp. tandoori spice powder
300g plain yoghurt
½ tbsp. ground cumin
30 leaves fresh mint

Instructions

Trim the salmon into cubes and coat with tandoori spice powder. Leave to
marinate in the fridge for 1 hour.

In a bowl mix 1/4 of the yoghurt with the chilli, mint, cumin, salt and
pepper and then place in the fridge.

Dice the tomato, peel and finely chop the onion and peel the cucumber and
dice.

Cook the salmon in the Actifry for 5 to 6 minutes (without oil).

Mix the chilli yoghurt with the remaining yoghurt, the tomato, cucumber
and the chopped onion.

Pour the sauce a small plate and top with the salmon.

Lamb Chops

Serve: 1
476 Calories per serving

Ingredients

2 Onions
4 Large Lamb chops
2 servings of frozen vegetables (not broccoli)

Instructions

Heat up the Actifry for 5 minutes, and then cut up an onion into slices and add them to the Actifry

After about a minute add the 4 large Lamb chops and cook for 25 minutes.

After 15 minutes add in another cut up onion.

Finally add 2 servings of frozen vegetables and cook for a further 3 minutes.

Serve with green vegetables

Spanish Style Squid

Serve: 2
402 Calories per serving

Ingredients

1 kg squid
1 tbsp. wheat flour
1 tbsp. olive oil
Garlic and parsley
Salt
2 tbsp. Garlic Mayonnaise to serve.

Instructions

Clean the squid and then season with salt and coat with flour.

Place the coated squid in the Actifry with the garlic and parsley, along with a spoon of olive oil.

Cook for 15 minutes and then serve with chopped spring onions and a garlic mayonnaise dip

Spanish Omelette

Serve: 2
313 Calories per serving

Ingredients

6g Serrano cured ham
1 green chilli
4 eggs
3 medium-size potatoes
A few parsley leaves
1 tbsp. olive oil

Instructions

Peel the potatoes, cut them into pieces and place them in the Actifry with the green chilli cut into strips.

Drizzle over the oil and cook for 20 minutes.

Cut the ham into small strips and add to the potatoes with the eggs and cook for another 5 minutes.

Decorate with a few parsley leaves.

Beef Stroganoff

Serve: 4
457 Calories per serving

Ingredients

500g tender beef
1 tbsp. vegetable oil
¾ cup chopped onions
1 tbsp. paprika
60ml sour cream
Salt and pepper

Instructions

Chop the beef and marinate it in a bowl with the paprika.

Heat the vegetable oil in the Actifry, and add the onions.

Cook for 5 minutes or until the onions are transparent, and then add the beef and cook for 3 to 4 minutes.

Finally add the sour cream and cook for a further 3 minutes.

Serve with vegetable pasta.

Grilled Coriander chicken

Serve: 6
357 Calories per serving

Ingredients

1 whole (about 1 kg) chicken - chopped into pieces
Juice of 5 small limes (2 cm in diameter each) (or to taste)
1 bulb garlic - peeled
50 g ginger - coarsely chopped
2 stalks lemongrass - coarsely chopped
1 red chili - coarsely chopped
50 g fresh coriander (include stem and roots) - coarsely chopped
2 tsp sugar
2 1/2 tbs fish sauce

Instructions

Place all ingredients except the chicken into a food processor and blend until fairly finely processed.

In a bowl, mix together the marinade and chicken, marinate for at least 1 hour, preferably overnight.

Put chicken pieces in the ActiFry and cook for 20 minutes.

Pour in the remaining marinade and continue cooking for another 10 minutes or until browned.

Serve with a little fresh coriander

Courgette crisps

Serve: 2
159 Calories per serving

Ingredients

600g thinly sliced courgette (about 2-3 medium)
2 tbsp. extra virgin olive oil
2 tbsp. white balsamic vinegar
2 tsp coarse sea salt

Instructions

Slice the courgette into really thin slices.

In a small bowl whisk together the olive oil and vinegar and add the courgette.

Add to the Actifry and sprinkle with sea salt.

Cook for 20 minutes or until they are crisp.

Chilli Chick Peas

Serve: 2
176 Calories per serving

Ingredients

205g tin drained chickpeas
1 tbsp. of oil of your choice
1 tsp chili powder
1tsp salt

Instructions

Drain the tin of chickpeas and rinse under water.

Place on several paper towels and dry well.

Add to Actifry along with oil, chili powder and salt and cook for 20 minutes.

Grilled tomato

Serve: 1
50g Calories per serving

Ingredients

2 Tomatoes
Herbs
Pepper
Cooking Spray

Instructions

Wash tomatoes and cut in half.

Turn all halves cut side up and spray lightly with frylight.

Sprinkle with ground black pepper and your choices of dried herb or
herbs.

Place tomato halves into Actifry cut-side up. And cook for 20 minutes.

Hunter Chicken

Serve: 4
297 Calories per serving

Ingredients

2 large chicken breasts, diced
2 sausages, chopped
4 rashers of streaky bacon cut into small strips
1 onion, diced
2 courgettes
100g of mushrooms
100ml Crème Fraiche
2 tbsp. wholegrain mustard
1 tsp honey
225ml dry cider
1 Halo spoon vegetable oil
1 tsp chopped rosemary
Salt & Pepper

Instructions

Add the diced onion to the Actifry and drizzle over a tbsp. of vegetable oil

Cook the onions for 5 minutes, or until they start to soften.

Add the chopped chicken, bacon and sausage to the Actifry, and cook for a further 15 minutes until the chicken begins to turn golden brown

Add the chopped rosemary and courgettes and mushrooms.

Next add in the mustard and honey followed by the cider.

Cook for 20 minutes or until the sauce begins to reduce.

Add in crème fraiche just before serving.

FREE COOKBOOK DOWNLOAD

25 low calorie curry recipes
for your slow cooker with
easy to follow instructions.
Delicious recipes

If you would like a free cookbook for your slow cooker, visit this link:
http://www.maryannemadden.com/slender-cookbooks

If you'd like more information about the Author, the Slender Cookbook
range, or about self-publishing cookbooks please visit:

www.Maryannemadden.com

Other Slender Cookbook titles

Slender Slow Cooker Cookbook

Delicious Low Calorie Recipes for Slow Cookers.

Slender Slow cooker Curry Cookbook

Available for FREE from www.maryannemadden.com/slender-cookbook

Coming soon...

Slender Halogen Oven Cookbook

Slender Soup Maker Cookbook

Slender Spiralizer Cookbook

JUST BEFORE YOU GO...

We'd be really grateful for a review on Amazon.

Thank you x

Made in the USA
San Bernardino, CA
26 July 2016